Some 12.000 years ago…

The Faca Stones,
Facatativá, Colombia

Santiago Martínez Concha

Some 12.000 years ago…
The Faca stones, Facatativá, Colombia.
Santiago Martínez Concha

Some 12.000 years ago…
The Faca stones, Facatativá, Colombia.

Santiago Martínez Concha

Some 12.000 years ago…
The Faca stones, Facatativá, Colombia.
Santiago Martínez Concha

Some 12.000 years ago…
The Faca stones, Facatativá, Colombia.
Santiago Martínez Concha
The Faca stones, Facatativá, Colombia.

The big head is that of a fish and the smallest that of a snake that emerges from the earth, both heads present an impressive realism. The largest head presents two eyes being the possible conjugation of two animals in only one - male- female? - It would be very interesting to excavate the earth around these figures in order to verify if they have bodies, as it was done with the Easter Island heads with amazing results, because until then no one knew with certainty the real and monumental size of the images. Are there buried bodies? Unfortunately, nobody seems interested and the budgets of the Colombian Institute of Anthropology is so scarce that is not enough for that.
Last degenerative stage.
-Author's photo-.

Some 12.000 years ago…
The Faca stones, Facatativá, Colombia.

Santiago Martínez Concha

If humanity is older than we think, then the Nephilim saw some of the greatest catastrophes of antiquity. Some of cosmic origin, as were any of the four massive extinctions lived during the last 440 million years. Three produced by planetary impacts or the last caused when the earth captured the moon in its orbit, - perhaps a Mars' twin planet - about 12 or 13,000 years ago bringing what we know as the Universal Flood. Not only did we steal the moon, Mars' twin planet, but perhaps its water as well. Other catastrophes of terrestrial origin, such as the eruption of Mount Toba 71,000 years ago, forced the earth to live through the coldest period of the Pleistocene or the Ice Age forcing earth's inhabitants to seek refuge in the depths of the earth in order to guarantee their survival.

Some 12.000 years ago…
The Faca stones, Facatativá, Colombia.
Santiago Martínez Concha

The Faca stones, Facatativá, Colombia.

Satan's head.

Satan's head. This impressive head in Facatativa it
weighs over 200l tons. When it is observed, the hair

twitches and its impressive realism can be seen. In the case of this incredible investigative adventure, everything that is affirmed in a simple and enjoyable language is shown with extraordinary photographs and graphic studies. Nothing is left to chance and without sufficient verification. In other words, it is a way of looking at the past with an open and fresh mind, putting the story back together with arguments of 'sufficient truth', 'erratic evidence', knowledge and dedication. This study not only teaches a new way of seeing the world and our antediluvian past, but it also breaks down existing theories and will not go unnoticed, becoming a must-read for many scholars and the general public. Scientists, historians, archaeologists, anthropologists and paleontologists will find here an extraordinary source of wealth for their future research, thanks to the findings, ingenuity, creativity and versatility of the findings.

-Author's photo-.

In Facativá exists -as a corollary- many other stones with fantastic heads and animals' bodies, which shows that malign mixture of fallen angels and the different species of the animal kingdom that populated the planet in those times, not only in Colombia but everywhere else in the world, stone images made thousands or millions of years ago with impressive realism as in the previous photo, although it is true no one knows how these sculptures were made and how big they are, because there are no resources to unearth them in their entirety. A very similar

case happened with the Easter Island sculptures, which only some were unearthed in their entirety, thus demonstrating whole body sizes much larger than expected and causing a worldwide stir.

It's been a while since I started the chain of my discoveries and I still cannot help but be surprised to see the plastic capacity of those Watchers and their children the Nephilim.

Note:

The legend that is most heard about these stones is that many years ago the priest who was building the Church of Facatativa finished the stone, which is why he had to stop construction, until one day the devil appeared and he proposed him a deal: "in exchange for the stone that you need to finish the church, you give me your soul". The father immediately accepted and that's how the devil, in the company of many of his subjects, begun bringing the stones, one after the other. Until one day it was so much the guilt and remorse that the priest felt, that he ended up regretting the deal, at that moment the devil was filled with anger and ordered to leave those stones lying there. But nobody knows in those places if that legend is true. Well, the truth is more terrifying

Some 12.000 years ago…
The Faca stones, Facatativá, Colombia.

Santiago Martínez Concha

than fiction and without a doubt, the fallen angels are connected with the devil and his henchmen. What we

will never understand is how they carved the different sculptures, some of them enormous, how long they lasted doing it, or, if they did it in an instant or in a single night. The legend also tells that the stones were taken from Tunja, a nearby town and that the demons moved them through the air on moonlit nights so that no one would notice. The transfer of images and buildings carried long distances by the angels as the house of the Virgin Mary which was carried by the good angels from the Holy Land to Loreto at night is well known. Another case in Colombia is the transfer of the picture of the Virgin of Monguí from Sogamoso to that place. It seems then that the angels do have that ability if God allows it.

The Faca stones, Facatativá, Colombia.

Some 12.000 years ago…
The Faca stones, Facatativá, Colombia.
Santiago Martínez Concha

Note 2: The Nephilim or giants, a race of warriors, to which rulers and Atlantean kings belonged, not only did not settle for having as many as they wanted from

the daughters of men, but their greed led them to seize the planet, leaving its marks and monuments everywhere, as if wanting to impose themselves on God's creation. On the other hand, their sexual appetite led them to transgress the same laws of nature and they "corrupted all flesh", and as it is written in the book of Enoch, maintaining relations with the fish of the sea, the birds of the sky and the animals of the earth. –Author's photo. –

A bird. -Author's

Note that I use the term animals and not beasts, because the Watchers and their children the Nephilim's corrupted all flesh and even that of many insects. They ended up

eating everything produced with the work of men. When the food was over, they continued eating the humans and drank their blood, but things did not end there, in the end they ended up eating themselves, also drinking their blood. And these, dear reader, were the real causes of having attracted God's punishment with the Great Universal Flood, because God **"hurt in His Heart,"** and repented of his creation. As much as Enoch interceded for them before, God's Throne, He did not forgive their sins and closed for them heaven's gates, decreeing their eternal condemnation and the destruction of their children -the Nephilim-.

The 200 damned angels led by Shemihaza who swore on the summit of Mount Hermon, decreeing that anyone who withdrew or turned against that covenant would be "anathema" or accursed among them. The angels being spiritual beings they did not die and they are still chained inside the earth or on its surface and they will be banished to hell the day of Last Judgment. This book shows with impressive photographs part of that tragedy and gives testimony of that which is

Some 12.000 years ago…
The Faca stones, Facatativá, Colombia.

Santiago Martínez Concha

narrated in the Bible and in the Book of Enoch. Everything said there is true and not a simple fable. Hence the teaching and warning for those who do not want to believe, because no one makes fun of God and while he is compassionate and merciful, the angels' sin is unforgivable because they

were created with pure intelligence, pure memory and pure will. Let us then return to God with a contrite and humiliated heart that He will not despise us.

Note:

Many of the antediluvian monuments of the Nephilim or their fathers the Watchers, are huge and were made to be seen from a distance or at high altitude depending on the sun and the position of the one who sees. Their capacity for abstraction is extraordinary. If we stick to the literal meaning of the word Nephilim, this, in Hebrew means "fallen". Their fathers were the Watchers or in other words refers to fallen angels. According to the Book of Enoch there were 200 and they had as leader one called Shemihaza. Being angels, it is not difficult to understand that they could fly or levitate and have immense power capable of achieving extraordinary feats, many of which we will see in this investigative compilation. Sometimes the figures carved into the rock intermingle with different meanings and were perhaps made over thousands and probably

Santiago Martínez Concha

millions of years. In many cases the male-female duality is expressed.

Dear reader, remember that, from space, the world can be viewed from any angle. Some years have passed since I began to explore the heads and figures that are on earth and I cannot stop being surprised. If the Nephilim did not make them who made them? Why did they do it? Was it

a desire for a whole kind of not to disappear for posterity? It is as if a competition between them had taken place. It is obvious that, given the complexity of the works, they were developed over long periods of time –or as I said elsewhere, were they done instantly? - In the case of the Suesca's heads, it can be observed how the sculptures of some were superimposed on those made by others. They did not want to waste a centimeter of the cliffs. Everything is sculpted. It is as if several painters and sculptors had worked for centuries on a canvas that in this case are the same rocks.

The faces we have seen and those we will see below, are an impressive and monumental testimony with tears frozen in stone, thousands of years old: As we have seen elsewhere, The Nephilim begged the prophet Enoch to intercede for them before the throne of God so that He would forgive them for their crimes and sins and allow

Some 12.000 years ago…
The Faca stones, Facatativá, Colombia.
Santiago Martínez Concha

them to enter Paradise, but God did not forgive them and He did not allow them to enter. This testimony of the crying of the Nephilim can be seen in almost all the photos in this book.

Some 12.000 years ago…
The Faca stones, Facatativá, Colombia.
Santiago Martínez Concha

Some 12.000 years ago…
The Faca stones, Facatativá, Colombia.
Santiago Martínez Concha

The Faca stones, Facatativá, Colombia.

A- Impressive pig's head and -B- fox's head. -Author's photo-.

Some 12.000 years ago…
The Faca stones, Facatativá, Colombia.
Santiago Martínez Concha

The "Faca stones", Facatativá, Colombia.

Nephilim's head holding a huge weight on itself - as if he were carrying the weight of his guilt - It is very interesting to observe the tears that roll down his cheeks and the sadness that overwhelms him for having lost Paradise. Observe that it has painted lips or darker, which makes it presume that perhaps it is a female. Last degenerative stage.
-Author's photo-.

Some 12.000 years ago…
The Faca stones, Facatativá, Colombia.
Santiago Martínez Concha

The "Faca stones", Facatativá, Colombia.

-1 and 2- The male-female duality. It impresses greatly the makeup of the female in the eyebrows and on her lips. That was something that little was known about of the costumes over 12,000 years ago. – Author's photo-.

Some 12.000 years ago…
The Faca stones, Facatativá, Colombia.
Santiago Martínez Concha

The "Faca stones", Facatativá, Colombia.

Head of an old man with a frown and impressive
realism. –Author's photo-.

Some 12.000 years ago…
The Faca stones, Facatativá, Colombia.
Santiago Martínez Concha

The "Faca stones", Facatativá, Colombia.

Snake's head. It is very interesting to observe the third dimension. People on it give scale to its huge size. The cavern below remains partially unexplored. Last degenerative stage.
-Author's photo-

Some 12.000 years ago…
The Faca stones, Facatativá, Colombia.
Santiago Martínez Concha

The "Faca stones", Facatativá, Colombia.

When I observed this great head, I felt the passage of centuries. I wonder how it lost its right eye. It seems that something or someone took it out of a slash -Author's photo-.

Some 12.000 years ago…
The Faca stones, Facatativá, Colombia.

Santiago Martínez Concha

The "Faca stones", Facatativá, Colombia.

This amazing Nephilim's head -1- resembles a gigantic stone sphere. It is covered with a kind of white paint or coating that in some cases are tears. His neck -2- presents two eyes which also cry white tears. –Author's photo-

Some 12.000 years ago…
The Faca stones, Facatativá, Colombia.
Santiago Martínez Concha

The "Faca stones", Facatativá, Colombia.

This huge head seems to be that of a dog - note the ear - however, I'm not sure what another animal it could be. The person who poses to give it scale is a friend who has decided to remain anonymous. – Author's photo-.

Some 12.000 years ago…
The Faca stones, Facatativá, Colombia.
Santiago Martínez Concha

The "Faca stones", Facatativá, Colombia.

−Author's photo-

Some 12.000 years ago…
The Faca stones, Facatativá, Colombia.
Santiago Martínez Concha

The "Faca stones", Facatativá, Colombia.

This horrendous head with a mocking smile and a
putrid mouth in terrible condition, has two lumps
like tumors on both eyes -Author's photo-.

Some 12.000 years ago…
The Faca stones, Facatativá, Colombia.
Santiago Martínez Concha

The "Faca stones", Facatativá, Colombia.

In this case, it seems that smallpox left its mark on the skin of this unfortunate victim, a victim who carry its pain from the time of the Great Flood. - Author's photo-.

Some 12.000 years ago…
The Faca stones, Facatativá, Colombia.
Santiago Martínez Concha

The "Faca stones", Facatativá, Colombia.

This incredible photograph shows a family group of a dog, his companion and a puppy. Everyone cries - even the puppy- But what is most moving is that they were not forgiven by God for their parents 'sin –the Watchers- transgressed His laws. - Author's photo-.

The "Faca stones", Facatativá, Colombia.

Here another animal appears, maybe another dog, also crying bitterly. -Author's photo-.

Some 12.000 years ago…
The Faca stones, Facatativá, Colombia.
Santiago Martínez Concha

The "Faca stones", Facatativá, Colombia.

In this photo, the Nephilim's mouth resembles a
bunker. The animal that partially hides the earth is
unidentifiable. Below, appears what it seems to be
the mouth of another unexplored head.
-Author's photo-.

Some 12.000 years ago…
The Faca stones, Facatativá, Colombia.
Santiago Martínez Concha

The "Faca stones", Facatativá, Colombia.

Yes, dear reader, I know that you are as amazed, impressed and overwhelmed as I am and have asked yourself a thousand questions that you have not been able to answer, but all this was written thousands of years ago and this is not simply believing but seeing. It is very interesting to observe also how without the need of the hands or bodies, facial expression suffices to denote feelings, emotions and actions. In the case of Figure -1-, it acts like the male and is above and behind the female -2-. Both heads cry copiously. - Author's photo-.

Some 12.000 years ago…
The Faca stones, Facatativá, Colombia.
Santiago Martínez Concha

The "Faca stones", Facatativá, Colombia.

Impressive worm or giant snake among the Faca stones, that also remembers the one that conforms the Island of Madagascar or the "megalodon" - or giant shark - in the Canary Islands, which the reader will be able to appreciate further ahead. These inclined stones pointing to heaven also seem to have a special meaning. -Author's photo-.

Some 12.000 years ago…
The Faca stones, Facatativá, Colombia.
Santiago Martínez Concha

The "Faca stones", Facatativá, Colombia.

-A- A salamander's body, -B-turtle. -Author's photo-

The "Faca stones", Facatativá, Colombia.

The face of the figure -A- I do not know to which
animal it corresponds. Maybe it refers to a human
head. In the picture - B- my 6-year-old son Andrés
appears moving a branch that hindered the photo. The
horrendous deformed head recalls those that can be
seen in the Great Lakes of the USA and the Dialogues
of Plato when he affirms that the Nephilim were
degenerating in their contact with the human ones and
in the end, they became evil and perverse.
-Author's photo-.

Some 12.000 years ago…
The Faca stones, Facatativá, Colombia.
Santiago Martínez Concha

The "Faca stones", Facatativá, Colombia.

The head -1- seems to refer to a black woman with
bulging lips and something on her head.
-Author's photo-.

Some 12.000 years ago…
The Faca stones, Facatativá, Colombia.
Santiago Martínez Concha

The "Faca stones", Facatativá, Colombia.

My son Andrés poses besides a huge head that has
been rusted by time in order
to give it scale. -Author's photo-.

Some 12.000 years ago…
The Faca stones, Facatativá, Colombia.
Santiago Martínez Concha

The "Faca stones", Facatativá, Colombia.

-A- and -B- are saurian heads of impressive realism. -Author's photo-.

Some 12.000 years ago…
The Faca stones, Facatativá, Colombia.
Santiago Martínez Concha

The "Faca stones", Facatativá, Colombia.

We had lunch that afternoon on a huge head of an animal similar to a rodent and we continue with our journey. In the figure. A- Two fox like animals can be seen, the dominant male on top of the female, as if to fecundate it. -Author's photo-.

Some 12.000 years ago…
The Faca stones, Facatativá, Colombia.
Santiago Martínez Concha

The "Faca stones", Facatativá, Colombia.

This huge Nephilim's head, as in many other cases,
conjugates two images, one in front and one in profile
that seems to be observing the landscape.
-Author's photo-.

Some 12.000 years ago…
The Faca stones, Facatativá, Colombia.
Santiago Martínez Concha

The "Faca stones", Facatativá, Colombia.

Suddenly, a little higher appeared another head
moved by sadness and despair, and had a face
covered in tears. -Author's photo-.

Some 12.000 years ago…
The Faca stones, Facatativá, Colombia.
Santiago Martínez Concha

The "Faca stones", Facatativá, Colombia.

-1- Impressive hound's head. -2- Monster of the lizard family. -Author's photo-.

Some 12.000 years ago…
The Faca stones, Facatativá, Colombia.
Santiago Martínez Concha

The "Faca stones", Facatativá, Colombia.

Strange head of an indeterminate animal.
-Author's photo-.

Some 12.000 years ago…
The Faca stones, Facatativá, Colombia.
Santiago Martínez Concha

The "Faca stones", Facatativá, Colombia.

-A- Pig's. head. -B- Indeterminate animal's head. -
Author's photo-.

Some 12.000 years ago…
The Faca stones, Facatativá, Colombia.
Santiago Martínez Concha

The "Faca stones", Facatativá, Colombia

Indeterminate animal's Head. A person or double head? -Author's photo-.

END OF BOOK 3

Made in the USA
Las Vegas, NV
28 January 2022

42486784R00026